Don't Give Away
The End

Valerie Norment Bruce

BookLeaf
Publishing

India | USA | UK

Presentation by *BookLeaf Publishing*

Web: www.bookleafpub.com

E-mail: info@bookleafpub.com

ISBN:9789360947286

First edition 2024

DEDICATION

To Jesse,

You taught me the true meaning of strength in vulnerability, the importance of living with purpose, and the beauty of cherishing every single moment. Though your voice has quieted, your influence resonates within me, encouraging me to pursue my dreams with the same passion and determination I had the greatest pleasure of seeing in you. Your legacy is a beacon that guides me through the darkest nights and the toughest storms. Thank you for your unwavering belief in me, and your infectious smile that could light up the gloomiest days. You may have left my sight, but never my heart. This work, a culmination of lessons learned and battles fought, is dedicated to you. May it serve as a testament to the incredible impact you've made on my life and on the lives of many others. Here's to you—my inspiration, my home my guiding star. Your memory and love will forever be a treasure cherished deeply within me.

Love Always,
Your Valerie

ACKNOWLEDGEMENT

In the creation of this work, a journey both challenging and rewarding, I have found myself reflecting on the immeasurable support and unwavering encouragement I received from those closest to me. It is with a full heart that I extend my deepest gratitude to my friends and family, who stood by me through the highs and lows, offering their shoulders to lean on, their hands to hold, and their hearts to understand. To my siblings, for the laughter and the endless support, thank you for being my first friends and lifelong confidants. To my friends, who have become family, your presence in my life is a gift I cherish deeply. Thank you for the late-night conversations, the shoulder to cry on, and the moments of joy we shared. Your encouragement, constructive criticism, and unwavering support have been instrumental in my journey. To those who lent an ear, shared advice, or simply sat with me in silence, your kindness has been a beacon of hope. A special thank you to Chrissy, who has guided and inspired me. Your wisdom and insights have been invaluable, shaping not only this work but my personal growth. And to those who touched my life in ways they may never fully understand, your impact has been profound. You have taught me resilience, empathy, and the beauty of being myself. This book is not just my story; it is a mosaic of love, tragedy, trauma, brutal honesty, and hope.

Forever grateful,
Val

PREFACE

I intend for my words to help those who need to heal do so. Even if the words bring tears, and sadness, it's in the sadness we start to live again. The tears are freedom and I want each of us to live freely from caged emotions and bottled-up feelings. I write from a place of childhood trauma, some I was always highly aware of and some that just came to light in the last few years. My words come from a life lived with diagnosed and misdiagnosed mental disorders, trauma, unbearable loss, and the greatest of love.

Table of Contents

In The Stars..*1*

Quiet Breaking..*2*

Shared Burdens..*3*

He...*4*

Unspoken Depths...*5*

I Am..*6*

Echoes Transformed......................................*7*

I Burn..*8*

We Wrestled With The Devil.............................*9*

The Absent..*11*

Honesty...*12*

But I pray you do not hate me for my honesty along the way....................................*12*

Steps of Redemption....................................*13*

Hope...*14*

Unswayed..*15*

Contentment...*16*

You Always Stay...*17*

God is in The Brokenness..............................*18*

Eternally Us..*19*

We Were...*20*

Knowing You This Way..................................*21*

Remembering...*22*

Deception..*23*

Always Remember This..................24

Not the Usual Goodbye.................. 25

I Let Grief In..................26

It's Time To Go..................28

Becoming.................. 29

As I Move On.................. 30

The Kind Heart.................. 31

The Truth.................. 32

Lucky me.................. 33

Our Melody..................34

I Sold My Wedding Dress..................36

Who Is She.................. 37

Timeless.................. 38

The In-between.................. 39

I Choose To.................. 40

YOU.................. 41

These Little Lights of Mine.................. 42

Superman.................. 43

Life Left to Go..................44

Growing Pains.................. 45

I Have Learned.................. 47

Lifelines.................. 48

Forever Neverland..................49

A Reunion of Sorrow and Truth.................. 50

The Wisest Man I Know.................. 52

The Answer.................. 53

JAKE..................54

It Was Everything............55

Trust............56

Light The Way............57

Reaching Out............58

Seeking Liberation............59

The Truth............60

The Dark Place I Go............61

I Wanted Different............62

What I Know To Be True............63

In The Stars

Lost love, not forgotten, but held above, in the
infinite expanse.
Each star is a memory, a moment we shared, a
testament in the heavens that you're still there.
So when the night unveils its starry glow, I look
up, and find you, in the expanse above.
Our love is not lost, but etched in the skies.

Quiet Breaking

2

Now, silence is my sanctuary it says so much
more than words ever could.
The sound of our laughter and those late-night
promises feel like they're from another lifetime.
A sweet song turned into a ghostly echo that
keeps me up at night.
In this stillness, I realize you're a chapter that
ended quietly but broke my heart into a million
loud pieces.

Shared Burdens

3

You could have shared, whispered your despair.
Told me the weight was too much to bear.
I carry the sorrows of others,
make them mine,
Would have shouldered yours, intertwined.

He

In his quiet, there's a kind of magic.
He's a calm force in all this static.
He loves me, flaws, and all, catches me, every
time I fall.
His hands might tremble, but his grip is strong,
He's the real deal.
Kindness with no end.
He shows me forgiveness, like an old-school
trend.
I'm a whirlwind, chaos at full blast, but next to
him, I find peace.
He's steady in all my storms and sees the real
me.
His love is so genuine; I pray it is true. He loves
me, and loving him back is all I want to do.

Unspoken Depths

5

Your silent look says it all, loud and clear.
Right next to me, your look spells out your
deepest desires.
Even when we don't speak, I get you, I really do.
As you keep moving, pretending the pressure
doesn't get to you. I've grown to respect the quiet
power you carry. I know that sometimes I ask
for more than I give back, but believe me, I see
the toll our journey takes on you. The challenges
we've faced have shaped you, just as they've
changed me. Now, more than ever, I realize
you're showing me who you really are, in all
your layers and depth.
Forgive me if I am running behind and I'm not
in that same place just yet.

I Am

In the quiet, I'm a whisper, a storm in the break,
A hunter in the shadows, a deer in the wake. I'm
the rhythm in the madness, the calm in the fray.
A lighthouse in your darkness, the night that
swallows day. I walk with assurance, yet tremble
in my skin. A puzzle with missing pieces, beauty
waiting to begin. I'm the stark contradiction, the
truth within the lie. A tale as old as time. With
every heartbeat, I'm writing my song, a melody
of me, where all the notes belong. I'm the light,
I'm the shadow, courage wrapped in fear. A story
you can read loud and clear.

Echoes Transformed

At first, I thought I was just your
echo—opposite sides of the same coin. I spent
way too long under the heavy quiet you threw. It
was so intense it almost felt like an attack on me.
But as time went on, I started to see through,
realized your world wasn't mine, broke free, and
grew.
Your beliefs don't box me in anymore, I've
moved past that stage.
No need for your okay, I'm setting my own pace.
Now, I'm aiming higher, my patience running
thin, got a determined fire burning bright within.
I'm on a new journey now, your silence can't
hold me back. For those coming next, remember,
our history's just a lesson, not a rule, go further.
It's time to break the silence, choose our own
paths, and live free, that's my choice.
I am finally using my voice.

I Burn

I'm burning and they say I'm to blame.
The thing they don't know is their words lit the flame.
It is in their judgment, misconception, and lack of understanding that I catch fire.
My fire rages but only on these pages.
I write in silent screams.
When I'm done crying in script
I emerge with a smile they equipped me with since I was a child.
They sit in silent approval while weighed down in denial.
And I continue to burn all the while.

We Wrestled With The Devil

In youth's innocence, the truth was veiled thin, A world harsh and cruel, where devils dwell within. Guardians stood by, eyes wide yet blind, As piece by piece, I fractured in their mind. A secret buried deep through silent years, unearthed in whispers, confirmed fears. The devil, they caged, with fleeting resolve, Not seeing the puzzle they needed to solve. He'd roam free again, this much I knew, yet I remained trapped, a reality askew. Did they see it? Was their protection merely a myth? A child lost to shadows, adrift. Now, it falls upon me, boundaries to trace, lines in the sand, in this desolate space. The girl that was taken, in fragments she lies, within me, she whispers, within me, she cries. Did they ponder, the woman she'd be? Not this shadowed self, not this fractured me. Together, we battle, she and I, weary of fighting, yet unwilling to die. For her, I rise, against our shared plight, standing firm, for us, I'll fight. We've danced with the devil, in the dark, unseen, In battles silent, where few have been. This struggle, ours, a story untold, A fight for the land, a reclaiming of soul. With each new

dawn, our resolve we mend, For I am
determined, this cycle will end.

10

The Absent

Why did the universe choose you, to take and not to borrow?
 Leaving me to navigate, what feels like an ocean of sorrow.
Your absence is a void.
In this universe without you, I lose myself each day.
I am haunted by the future, the plans that will never be, and the crippling weight of the question, why did you have to leave?
 So, I wander through our memories, a ghost when I am in your home.
I find myself whispering to the shadows, feeling more alone.
The world moves on around me, but I'm stuck in our past.
 In the stillness of the night, with tears that never dry, my soul reaches for yours, still asking, "Why?"

Honesty

I know you are trying hard to hold on.
While I hold out strong.
But we set ourselves down for so long.
And if I am honest I am uncertain this is where
we belong.
How do we undo the mess we have become?
I watch you carry a weight that doesn't belong to
you.
It is the same thing I always do.
I realize we are the same in so many ways.
In time
Maybe
We will get back to you and me

But I pray you do not hate me for my honesty along the way.

Steps of Redemption

13

Each turn I took, every time,
A dance, a step out of line.
Burdens gathered, not mine to own,
Yet carried, in silence, alone.
Here I stand, releasing the weight,
Forgiving myself, before it's too late.
For every stumble, every fall, I rise, I learn,
embracing it all.

Hope

They say I'm naive, that I'm wasting my breath,
but if love can't save us, what hope do we have
left? So, I stand by you, through the highs and
the lows, believing in the person that nobody
knows.
 For love is a beacon in the darkest night, and I'll
hold onto you, with all of my might.
They may never understand why I choose to
fight, but I have always seen your worth and
your inner light.
If love can be salvation, a reason to strive, then
I'll walk this path with you, as long as I'm alive.
For the heart has reasons, some reasons we do
not know, and where it leads us, only love can
show. So here I am, with hope as my guide,
forever believing in us, with love on our side.

Unswayed

I embrace their misunderstanding, and let it
stand, In their realm of error, uncorrected,
unplanned.
My strength lies in serenity, in the deep knowing
that this path was mine, rightly chosen, not
cheap.
The bridges were aflame, in hindsight, a
beautiful blaze, Illuminating my journey through
life's intricate maze. For every fire walked
through, every ember that seared,
crafted the soul I am now, the one that
persevered.

Contentment

I've ceased to trust in mere chance, now
understanding the essence of reality.
It is my reservoir of patience, not my love, that
has depleted.
I'm solitary yet content, but jaded. I live these
fantasies, I transcend, and from this view, I find
pure joy.

You Always Stay

17

You found me shining, at the peak of my game,
then watched as the storm clouds came.
But you, you chose to stay, drawing me closer,
come what may.
You never once thought of walking away, even
on my darkest day.
Someday, I'll find a way to show gratitude for
your love's glow.
You are the best friend I have ever known.

God is in The Brokenness

No shame in my past, no shadows cast,
For each misstep, each trial amassed,
Has sculpted me, bold and unashamed,
Proud of the soul I've reclaimed.
Come, draw near, share this space,
Let me unfold the grace in disgrace.
Sit by my side, lend me your ear,
Hear of the wonders when God draws near.
In every break, every tear, every scar,
Lies a story of how great His mercies are.

Eternally Us

We were unstoppable, pure dynamite, pure
magic.
We had the world at our feet amidst the chaos.
Shining bright, like neon against the
monochrome.
We were the stuff of legends; being with you
was pure bliss.
We took the long way around and finally
admitted what we already knew.
We lived on the edge, a mix of tragedy, epic
moments, and sheer brilliance.
 I'll forever cherish the love you gave me no one
else was privy to; we're eternally etched in the
sands of time.
This is a legacy to be remembered, a story
penned in permanent ink. Through every storm
and challenge, we were always going to take it
on unphased.
Through time our story will always prevail.
In the end, we crafted our own epic tale.

We Were

We knew the dance, the steps, and the rhythm
woven into memories from times when distance
was our middle name. I said, "Time heals," but I
was cautious, not wanting to be blinded by the
stars. Yet, in your light, I felt something
unprecedented, unmatched, if a single glance
spells legend, then we're immortal.
From a kiss to talks of forever, living on
borrowed time, flirting with eternity, our love
was never fully alive or dead because you were a
paradox of a man. Your confessions were holy
yet so human.
I've never felt such emptiness. Your words were
a maze of a future planned.
 I wonder sometimes if they cringe at my
naivety. Promises of never leaving quickly
turned to dust. Our dreamscape is now ashes,
your departure unexplained.
We are a vision that will haunt me until my
dying day.

Knowing You This Way

21

Discovering you, as you stand today,
Feels like my favorite track, hitting play.
A melody reborn, a fresh embrace, like a
timeless tune, in a brand new space.
It's the thrill of the drop, the chorus we know,
but yet it hits differently because we are so.
A familiar beat, under a new light,
Dancing to the rhythm feels just right. You, a
song I've loved, now with a twist. This remix of
a classic is too good to resist.

Remembering

22

Reminding myself that
Your voice won't grace my ears
Until we meet beyond the stars
Feels like an echo of hell in my memories.

Deception

My dear,

Your attempts at gaslighting me have become
my favorite form of flattery.

Try as you might, I'm aware of the light.

Always Remember This

He knew you stood so near, in shadows and in light. With every act, every gesture, it was clear. All that could be, in love, was done, in every setting sun, every rising one.
Love, a beacon, steady and aware. He knew that in every breath, deep, unwavering love was always there.

Not the Usual Goodbye

25

His farewell was unlike any other.
No embrace
No kiss
Not even a simple wave.
It was a goodbye that resonated in silence,
Lasting forever.
The kind that leaves a mark, eliciting more than
just tears.
I live in an everlasting state of missing your
embrace and despair without you here.

I Let Grief In

Grief knocked, and I hesitated but let it in.
It sat down like an old friend.

There were visits before, but just a pass-through
and nothing more.

This visit is new.
This time, it's different; it won't leave.

This loss was unexpected, and the love that died,
too, was something so true.
It's hard to describe or understand, and grief just
stares at me like I know where to begin.
I don't know what to do, so I beg grief to walk
me through the steps. It is time to start; it's been
months since your departure. But grief sits
quietly, waiting for something I'm unaware of.

I finally asked it to leave

Maybe it's just not meant to be here with me, but
instead, it is starting to move closer to me.

It begins to speak in delicate, painful memories.
I am so angry that it gets to do this to me.

It's too much, I've had enough. I stop here and
demand it to leave.
After I had closed the door I turned around to
see grief still sitting there waiting for me.
I'm terrified to see this through, as terrified
as I am to go on without you.

It's Time To Go

In realms where my presence was not destined to thrive, I lingered, so willingly, so naively alive.
Beauty veiled the darkest secrets in its embrace, Whispering tales in spaces where light scarcely graced.
The road less traveled, with its mysterious allure, summoned my soul.
Yet, amidst the wanderlust, a clear vision arose—the sanctuaries calling, where my spirit truly knows.
Places that promise healing, a return to wholeness welcome me without conditions, speaking to my soul. In their silent invitation, a truth brightly shone, a recognition of where my heart is truly known.
Now, with eyes wide open, I acknowledge the sign, that it is time to go.

Becoming

In quiet moments, I ponder my unseen face, had trauma not chosen me, an innocent in its embrace.
What roads remain untraveled, and what joys remain unlearned? Would my spirit have burned less fiercely? Might carefree laughter have been my song? Would life's weight have been perceived as less heavy and less long? Would the world's colors blend softer and less bright? Would my love's depth have found lesser light? Yet, in this contemplation, a truth softly speaks: a battle within, seeking its own peace. Now, as I journey through healing, I am curious about the self that will stand. May the change be kind, the growth true, retaining some essence of what I always knew.

As I Move On

In the quiet of the morning, I feel you all around,
but it's time to face the daylight with my feet on
solid ground.
I've been holding onto shadows, living in our
yesterday, but the whispers of the dawn, say it's
time to find my way. So, I'm letting go, but I'll
keep you in my heart. A love that's passed, but
will never truly part. With every step I take,
you're my guiding star. I have the map I know
exactly where you are.
I see you in the sunset, in the colors of the sky
knowing hues of orange were your favorite I
now understand why. I've been walking through
this world, feeling lost without you here, but I
know you'd want me smiling, living life beyond
my fears.

The Kind Heart

That soul you know, who loves with depth so bold, holds compassion vast, for stories left untold. A gentleness in their being, a softness in their gaze, finding specks of light on the darkest of days. Tread gently around them, hold them dear, for their journey's been long, their battles severe. They've seen life's harshest, faced its cruel jest, climbed from abysses, unspoken, a mess. Meeting you with kindness, on whatever path you roam, in their light, find a beacon, a guidepost, a home. Question not the brilliance of their inner glow, but cherish the struggle and the resilience they show. Embrace them whole, for the wars they've quietly weathered, for in their fight, a luminous spirit was gathered.

The Truth

"I'm okay," I whisper, but my soul is still littered
with shards. "I'm fine," I claim, but I'm
drowning under grief's weight. Though I was a
survivor, navigating through life's inferno, here I
am, crumbling into ash, more fragile than ever.
Dropping the facade and showing the real me
unveils a truth, a hidden version of myself,
imprisoned by pain and shadows. I'm not free,
trapped in this gloom, lying in bed, room
spinning, tears shed for you.
When I venture outside, I wear a smile like a
mask—a disguise for my tears—hoping no one
sees the sadness in my eyes. I exist, searching
for peace for my soul, sending prayers for a
change, for someone to turn this darkness into
dawn. I am desperate to understand, for a path to
keep going. At this moment, it's about surviving,
enduring the sting of a heartbreak's cruel cut.

Lucky me

I heard them speak, praise heaped upon his strength, for loving me in my wild streak. A marvel, they say, at length. "Fortunate," they whisper, as if luck played any part in love's chaotic dance. In my youth, their words struck, "Grateful," they said, for a chance. Not every kin turns the predator in, especially when he's woven into the family's skin. Years have passed, tears have dried, still,
"Lucky," they sigh, misguided pride. But luck has no place in this tale of mine, in a world where healing is a damn steep climb. At my peak, I'm a mosaic of scars and stories, gathering myself, in all my fragmentary glories. Lucky? No, that word doesn't fit, it's in resilience and rebirth this me you now see. A survivor, not by chance, but by fierce decree, crafting my destiny, breaking free. So, when they speak of luck and fate, I smile, knowing I've opened my own gate. Not lucky, but brave, in every step I take, in every piece I reclaim, every chain I break.

Our Melody

From Jack's and Straylight to ruining "Black
Balloon" for me, but, in all fairness, it was my
naivety. We always escaped into the music so
quickly.
From different cities, you would count down
from three, and we were on a "Champagne
High" simultaneously. I wonder if you remember
that car ride to Kim's when we lost all track of
time between The Beach Boys and Calvin
Harris. I remember "All Too Well." I'm still not
sure if you started an argument that one day so
we could have our own unrehearsed kitchen
scene.
I can't forget how you laughed when I knew so
many facts about a short film, or how you gave
in and watched it. I must skip over Death Cab
now because it turns out I couldn't "Follow You
into the Dark," and I'm not over that lie they
sang to me.
How true it was that everyone knew us and yet
knew nothing about us. Oh, the "Dress", and
"What a Cruel Summer" it turned out to be. Was
it two or three times you played "Hey Leonardo"
last Wednesday until I finally listened? I close
my eyes and smile when it comes on now, but I

can't sing along. I find too much irony now
when listening to Nothing But Thieves tell me,
"We don't always get all that we want."
Twenty-something years of us swapping songs
like we did secrets. I'll forever keep the last
playlist you sent to me; it spelled everything out
so perfectly. And that last Saturday night, how
you held me is seared in my memory. It was the
perfect moment while you played Mat and sang
in sync; "We don't need to waste that time
anymore. I never really felt this way before."
I'd give anything to hear you sing to me one
more time.
Sing to me…
sing
me
anything

I Sold My Wedding Dress

I nodded to a day dressed in splendor, a masquerade, with smiles wide and tender.
Donned my finest mask, a practiced art, I played my perfect part in that guise. An heirloom, this facade, worn with grace, a tradition I vowed to displace.
I'll bury its legacy deep into the earth. There will be no more secrets for my kin to keep. For I wasn't alone in this grand charade. There were masks all around, in this parade.
Time unwound, the truth emerged, unveiling the facade and leaving nothing but dust. If that dress crossed my path, scissors in hand, I'd take a piece to understand.
Under a different glow, might it reveal, a story different, a contrasting appeal?
The veil remains with me, a ghostly sheath, transparent, with a truth underneath. It reminds me of what was meant to be pure, yet in clarity, we find the allure.

Who Is She

I'm over it, the sight of her, that plastered grin, a blur. Her joy, a crafted tale, spread wide, living for others, herself aside. Their choices weighed, a growing wrath. It's a dance, her compliance, a sight to behold, "Are you enchanted?" I want to be bold. When weariness seeps, she sparks to life, a rebel at heart, amidst the strife. Flames rise, a silent scream, those fires, I ponder, their purpose unclear, burning brightest when she's near. Perhaps, in the mirror's gaze, I'll dare to inquire, if courage finds me, amidst our fire. To understand our quest, in a quiet plea, and remind the reflection, we're not made to flee. Not fireproof, yet still we ignite, hoping, maybe, we'll get it right. Or maybe we'll burn us down just in spite.

Timeless

I like to think right now in another reality
It's you and me
That our lives are easy
We're happy
The challenges of this life are nowhere in sight
We're watching our dreams come true
Everything we spoke about
The life we planned out
I have no doubt

In every lifetime
You are meant to be mine
And I am forever yours

The In-between

39

The toughest battle I have ever faced was the
clash between my knowledge and emotions.

I Choose To

You wonder, perplexed, how love found its way
to you, seeking in my gaze a clue, a reason that
was true. Your eyes hunt for concrete, graspable
reason, something a mind, enwrapped in beauty,
can't ignore.
With all the honesty that my heart can pour, I
say, "I choose to," a simple truth at its core.
You claim your luster's faded, not what it was
before, my darling, your gold was never what I
adored. To me, you've never dimmed, never lost
your gleam, despite your efforts. Even in the
night's embrace, where no light seems to beam,
you illuminate my existence.
Were you to ask once more the reason for my
love's ever-present presence, my answer would
remain unchanged, now and forevermore. "I
choose to," I restate with conviction, with every
fiber, a choice beyond reason. This was our fate.
For in the realm of love, where the heart
navigates, it's choice, not chance, that our bond
never broke. And as we sit here, I can see you
believe in all that's been revealed this year and
the very reason why we ended up here.

YOU

I survived you.
What a brave thing to do.
What a shame I had to.
Going forward, just know that I refuse to dilute
my essence to suit your palate. If it's too much
for you, you're welcome to struggle.

These Little Lights of Mine

42

Two little lights bestowed from the heavens
gleam so brightly in my heart. Uncertain I stand,
of who I'd be, without their luminescence,
setting me free. Their glow, a beacon in my
darkest night, guiding my steps, making the
heavy light. Gratitude for their shine, words can't
express.
In their brilliant beams, I find my way. A
profound blessing, in the purest display, God
graced my life in the most beautiful way.
I thank him each day for my two loving boys
and the way they saved me.

Superman

43

Your smile lit up the room like a song with its own tune; your knowledge was deep and bold, never shy. In a crowd, it was you I'd spot, your presence spoke more than words could plot.
I was filled with pride for all that was: the obstacles you hurdled, your fearless stance, the battles you fought, hidden inside, your unmatched bravery, a strength that never died. Through it all, you stood so firm, a symbol of courage in every term.
I've always been so proud of you, and I truly hope you felt that too.

Life Left to Go

There's still so much life ahead to explore, had I known then all I know now, at my core, I'd still choose the same path, not altering the score, for every moment was destined, part of the lore.

I feel shortchanged when I define "us." Had we seen from day one those destined to leave a scar, we'd not have grown into the beings that we are. We'd lack the depth, resilience, and richness we've shown, not reaching this far.

Both the joys and the sorrows, the journey through, the missteps and triumphs, the old and the new. I'm set on the paths that lie ahead, embracing life, no matter where I'm led. Eager for what's to come, the chapters yet to see, hoping they will find fragments of you reflected in me.

Growing Pains

She made a joke out of nothing at all.
Forcing fake joy because there was truly none to
be.
With just a glance, a smile so small, she turned
the world into comedy.
But these were manic turns from sad to happy.
Stories she chose to believe.
Lies she lived.
Still such good advice she had to give.
She would sit and write of things she was to do
knowing all too well she would not follow
through.
As comical and present as she could be she was
also the darkest thing you have ever seen.
As she got older, she finally grew to understand
that humor fits in sadness hand.
And her humor came from the tragedy she
defined herself by.
Somehow realizing this made her feel more alive
and now gave her the power to thrive knowing
this secret she didn't before.
She still makes jokes out of nothing and calls up
fake joy to get through some days.

Just know that she is able to see reality now in quite a different way, and her disconnect lessens each day.

I Have Learned

47

As I've gotten older, I've realized—stories aren't just black and white. I've got scars that are still healing, hard lessons learned through tough times, and doors I've closed on past chapters of my life... Goodbyes I've whispered to people I once held close. I've found out the hard way that proximity doesn't mean closeness. They say blood is thicker, but sometimes, connections run deeper. My inner circle is smaller now, but it's solid and full of strength. Experience has shown me, through setbacks and rejections, who I'll open my heart to and who I'll keep at a distance. The warmth of my home is carefully chosen, decorated with the wisdom of experience, knowing now, who'll be welcomed with open arms, and who'll never step beyond my doorway.

Lifelines

Thunderstorm at dawns
Coffee meetups at noon
Stargazing sessions at midnight
Cozy naps under soft blankets
Books that touch the heart
Embraces that reach deep into the soul
Conversations that last into the early hours
Secrets kept safe between us
Wildflowers picked from your sister's garden
The perfect cuddle
Those exclusive nights that are just ours
Deep discussions that matter
Daytime sightings of owls
A playlist that withstands the ages
The sound of strumming guitar strings
These are the things that keep me going

I count myself fortunate to have had you as one
of them, even if just for a while.

Forever Neverland

Reading the final chapter of our story, I can't help but smile through the tears. Now, everything makes sense - the years that once baffled me are clear. Every moment, every word, was a stitch in the fabric of our connection. The laughter that filled our days, the serious conversations we faced head-on, the memento you saved as a reminder that the only way out was through. We were reshaped, and refined by every challenge, and every hurdle. Our love, once vibrant in spoken words, now quietly concludes. Preserved in its essence, timeless and true. This isn't about Peter parting with Wendy or growing apart, in our own Neverland, we remain, caught in a timeless dance. Here in our story's epilogue, where fantasies and reality weave together, in Neverland, our spirits eternally drift.

A Reunion of Sorrow and Truth

In the quiet, reflective light of the chapel, old friends and distant acquaintances gather. Faces from the past, connected by time and now by loss. Years have flown, conversations paused, leaving a connection frayed yet not severed. Among them, some knew his beautiful soul intimately and could recount endless stories of joy and tears. Others swept up in the rush of life, find themselves here, reconnecting.

Eyes heavy with tears not yet fallen, each look serves as a bridge over lost time. They reminisce about days filled with laughter, now seen through a nostalgic glow. Close friends share in soft tones, tales that warm the soul, painting a picture of a life rich and full—a tapestry of adventures, love, and challenges, depicting the departed as family, lover, and friend.

In this gathering, something heals—a recognition that love, that true bonds, withstand the test of time. As the ceremony dims a silent vow forms among them. Despite life's divergent paths and the swift passage of years, such moments promise reunion and reflection. Leaving the chapel, they carry a piece of history, a shared sorrow that binds them indelibly. United in their loss, they step forward, hoping to remember the value of connection, the price of silence.

The Wisest Man I Know

In the depths of my despair, a wise man once told me, "It hurts because he was your choice," and there was so much truth in those words. His words, cut through my grief with a moment of clarity. This loss carved a unique path through us, binding us with the memory of a person who lit up our lives. Despite his own heartache, he was there with me, guiding me through the sorrow.

He helped me understand the depth of connections we choose, and the profound grief that can come with them. Ever since, I've made my choices more thoughtfully, aware of how deep the sting of loss can be. I'm grateful for the perspective he shared on making choices, on loss, and on finding courage. I wish I could thank him, if only words were enough, hoping to reflect his insight, no matter what comes.

The Answer

To feel the love, beyond your grasp, you yearned, to witness its flames, in your world, finally burn.

We defied the cosmic rule, the pull apart. Yet, in this dissonance, there is a question mark. Was I merely a shadow in your vibrant scene, a diversion from the path, or something in between?

I'd voice my doubts loud for you to hear. For in the depths where truths are often spun, you told me you realized I was always the one. When you asked a question to the Lord above, somehow, the truth was always revealed in my love. I knew the struggle you had with that, for honestly, I always had to. If I am honest with myself I still do.

JAKE

Through heartbreaks and trials, you've been my guide, a sister of choice, forever by my side. Not all bound by blood yet undeniably tied, I find family in you. If souls come in pairs, split at life's start, then surely, we're halves of the same heart. In every universe, apart or together, Best friends, us two, now and forever.

It Was Everything

55

Discovering the past didn't matter, its whispers silent and benign, You revealed a truth, a path I was designed to align. With clear vision and belief, you erased the past, free from hesitation, leaving behind the shadows cast. In your bold words, a commitment was born, No need for extravagance in our world, so simply adorned. Just being there was enough, a solid vow. Chasing perfection wasn't the goal; it was about the now. Together, we shone, defining what once was unclear, crafting moments precious, in our bond so dear. You are the epitome of decisions I've joyously made, Yet, you're also the deepest gap, a shadow that never fades. In the intricate weave of love, where lives entangle and break, you're my boldest choice and the sorrow I can't shake.

Trust

56

Broken trust is a painful teacher, guiding us to become our own healers. In the rubble, a new dawn's light, a chance to love, to live, to write. A journey begins with a single step, through the tears wept and promises kept. From broken trust, the heart learns self-healing, in the ruins, finding a second chance.

Light The Way

In those silent moments, my mind wanders, to a place where maybe your pain transfers. What if a different path, wide and smooth, was your choice, would it have lessened the weight, given you voice? But that rough, tangled road led to me, in this twisted fate, I came to be. I'm forever thankful for this twist of fate, Yet, this thought makes my heart hesitate: I'd give up everything, my essence, my all, if it meant you'd stand tall. To rewrite your story, to brighten your day, I'd willingly give my place away. In the economy of existence, affection, and moments, I'd cover your debts. To hand you a life, fresh and renewed, a gesture, for the depth of love I have for you two.

Reaching Out

58

My honesty wasn't meant to tear things down. It was there to bridge the gap you constantly seemed to miss. And after pouring my thoughts onto all these pages, I really hope you get it, because it took everything in me to try and connect with you.

Seeking Liberation

59

I'm not chasing disasters, just searching for what's mine. Yet here I am, boxed in, tagged a traitor by their design. For ideas they clutch, to which I'm utterly blind, never caught my interest, nor did they ever bind. So, how do I break out from this unfairly drawn line? A verdict dropped on my life, without a chance to decline. Do I keep my pride low, and just go with the flow, or find solace in the shadows, where whispers grow? Walking away from their judgment, their guilt, their endless play, tired of their blame game, the roles they want me to portray. Sick of being a puppet in battles I never chose to fight; caught in the crossfire of what they claim is wrong or right. How do I liberate myself, and step out of this relentless rain? Shake off their "my way or highway" chain? Escape this cycle, confusing and strained, and find my peace, finally unchained.

The Truth

It's not the truth that hurts us, but the realization that it's actually reality that scars us.

The Dark Place I Go

Sorting through my own mess, I search for some quiet, pulling back into myself, it's my way of fighting. When I am quiet, just get that I'm diving deep inside, wondering if I'm planning ahead or just along for the ride, caught in a space where I'm just figuring it out. But remember, I've got this cycle down, no doubt, coming back stronger, stepping out from the shadows. I've got the art of faking a smile down, hiding my lows. In the silence, I'm working through my inner chaos, piecing together my life's puzzle. So, if I seem to disappear, just know I'm on my way, finding my path back, a little wiser.

I Wanted Different

I've come to know the shadows that you lament. August memories, promises like ghosts, if truth be told, you've grown more complex, harder to hold. Rumors fly, whispers that you've found your crown, yet, I'm caught in thoughts, why you won't put it down. I harbored dreams of mending, but the rift remains wide, still ponder why maturity seems to slide. Hoped for days beyond these recurring scenes, Is it naive to wish for what could have been? Messages lost in the void, echoes of a plea; in the debris of us, is that where you'll be? A path diverged, in your labyrinthine ways. Once thought I could be the cure, a naive belief, stuck on the notion of change, now met with grief. Hoped we'd outgrow the storms, and leave them in our wake, yet here we stand, the same mistakes we remake. Is it futile, my wish for you to find your sun, to see you grow, to see you win?

What I Know To Be True

Underneath the towering shadows of past giants,
Inherited tales of darkness, quiet and compliant.
A heart once wide open, now silently bears the
age-old burden of unspoken despairs. Hidden
deep, roots of trauma wind and weave, through
the lineage, a pattern no one chose to receive. A
garden of grief, where nightmares take shape,
silently thriving in the night's dark drape. Yet, in
this darkness, a single spark dares to live. A
small beacon of hope, persistently positive.
Healing comes with time, and love standing by.
Proving that even the deepest cuts eventually
dry. Not just surviving, as if by some cosmic
mistake, but thriving, breaking free, a new life to
partake. Rising from sorrow, like a phoenix in
flight, wearing scars proudly, a testament to the
fight. Life's a winding road, with lessons at
every bend; a journey of healing, a broken heart
to mend. Though shadows of giants may darken
the way, the brilliance of resilience turns night
into day.
So here stands the survivor, bold and new,
crafting a path, with a vibrant hue. Transforming
trauma, into strength untold, a story of survival,
courageously bold.